ABOUT FACE

"A Soldier's Story" About Life, Resilience and Success
(A Memoir by)

Thomas Edward Taylor

Copyright © 2019 Thomas Edward Taylor

All rights reserved. No part of this book may be reproduced in any form or by any electronic or mechanical means, including information storage and retrieval systems, without permission in writing from the publisher, except by reviewers, who may quote brief passages in a review.

Library of Congress Control Number: 2019910188

Printed in the United States of America

First Printed Edition 2019.

Published by Amazon.com

Physical address or email: Thomastaylor31@gmail.com

Visit www.thomastaylor.net

Thomas Edward Taylor
P.O. Box 1060
Antioch, Tennessee 37011

ABOUT FACE

This memoir is dedicated to my Family, Friends, the United States Army and Army National Guard. Without You, I would not be where I am today. I also, want to give praise to my Lord and Savior Jesus Christ for giving me the strength and guidance to write this memoir. Thank you for teaching me that my attitude always determines my altitude.

Contents

DEDICATION 3
INTRODUCTION 5
1 Just A Small Town Boy 8
2 Becoming Part Of Something Much Bigger 12
3 My Big Decision Point 17
4 High School Graduation And My Misfortune 23
5 Embrace The Suck; You're In The Army Now! 30
6 That Good Ole Army Training: Drill Sergeant! 35
7 Not My Soda Can Drill Sergeant! 41
8 Germany, Here I Come 44
9 The Darkest Day Of My Life 50
10 The Courage To Come Forward 53
11 A Mother's Love And Understanding 58
12 Acceptance And Forgiveness 60
13 The End Of My Enlistment 62
14 You Need To Sweep That Floor, Sergeant! 65
15 The First Deployment (Saudi Arabia) 68
16 Two More Deployments 72
17 The Reality Of War 77
18 Transition Back To Civilian Life 79
CONCLUSION 84

INTRODUCTION
My Soldier's Story

I finally did it. I've finally written and self-published my memoir. Some may call it an autobiography or even a book. It's something that I've wanted to do for years. I feel as though I have only just begun to live this great circle of life. I want to share my story and leave a legacy to the next generation of my family to read.

Most of my life has been concentrated around the military; I was a Soldier, and now a Veteran. I served my country for thirty-six years, which included three deployments. I enlisted in the military right after graduation from high school. My life of selfless service helped to shape me into the person I am today. The military gave me the courage to overcome my fears and step out of my comfort zone. I hope that by sharing my story, it may inspire or convince others to do the same throughout their journey of life. I will explain military jargon used in this memoir for readers who have not served in the military, so they can gain a better understanding of my story.

Within these pages, you will find my story of small and humble beginnings, as a shy and introverted farm boy with wanderlust who left the family farm behind to proudly wear his country's uniform and become a man. You'll also journey with me through basic training, deployments, and ultimately, retirement from the military. I will also share my tumultuous transition from military to civilian life, starting my own business, going back to school and returning to the civilian workforce. I hope to share life lessons I've learned throughout life, in hopes that it may be useful to someone. One life lesson, do something that will take you out of your comfort zone and force you to conquer your fears. One of my fears was to go skydiving. After I retired from the military, I came out of my comfort zone and went skydiving. I conquered that fear. Challenge yourself to new heights. I challenged myself to ride a thousand miles on my Bianchi "The Green Machine" Road Bike. I accomplished that challenge in 2018.

This book will also tackle a heavy subject matter which is prevalent today in the Armed Services, "Military Sexual Assault." It isn't for the faint of heart, but it must be addressed. Sexual assault is a tragic reality in our world and in the military. It can happen to both men and women. Sexual Assault can happen to anyone, and all too often, victims are persuaded, bullied, or threatened into staying silent. I am going to share with you, my own story of being a victim of Sexual Assault while serving in the military. It took me some time to come to grips with it and to openly talk about it. I finally realized being a victim of sexual assault is nothing to be ashamed about. When victims stay silent, it only protects the perpetrators. Even when it is hard speaking up; it's the right thing to do. It saddens me when people don't believe you when you are a victim of sexual assault. You can never remember all the details. But what you do remember is what happen to you, where you were, and how you felt. That is what **We** remember.

I want to end this introduction by telling you just how honored and blessed I am to have been allowed to serve our great nation, "The United States of America." I want to give a special thanks to all Soldiers, Sailors, Marines, Airmen, Coast Guard, and Civilians who are currently serving, and to those who have served. Most importantly to those who have paid the ultimate sacrifice for our freedom; to those honorable Soldiers and their families, I salute you!

As we say in the army: a big *HooAh!* I hope you enjoy the memoir. Here is my story, a Soldier's story.

CHAPTER 1

Just A Small Town Boy

April 27, 1963, is the day that I was born to my mother, Dottie (or 'Mozelle,' as she is better known) Taylor, and my father, Thomas Eugene Taylor. I joined the world at the Lincoln County Hospital in Fayetteville, Tennessee. My parents named me Thomas Edward Taylor. I was almost a junior. I had a normal childhood, and my upbringing was full of happiness and love from my parents.

I grew up on the "family farm" as my father coined it, in a modest middle-class family. Farming was everything to him; owing farmland back then was considered a major accomplishment in Fayetteville for blacks. My father envisioned passing the farm down to his children when he passed away. I came from a decent-sized family; there were four kids altogether; along with me, there was my brother, Robert, and my two sisters, Dottie and Evelena. My siblings and I were always close. And, just like normal kids, we came up with nicknames, we called each other. We sometimes jokingly call each other those names today, of course with laughter and reminiscent. The three of them had a significant influence on my life, and I still love and care for them today as much as I did back then.

All four of us were sometimes picked on at school. The other kids would call us "country" because we lived out on a farm, in an area that was more rural than many of their homes. It's ironic, because I ended up traveling the world, and many of those same people who teased us ended up raising their kids out in the country. I suppose they eventually found the charm of country living after all. It didn't help us back then though when we were just trying to get through the school day without a problem.

Worse than the teasing we got for being the children of farmers was the racism. During the sixties and seventies in the South, attitudes weren't always the most progressive or accepting as it is today. In fact, they were often the opposite.

I remember one time, riding home on the school bus with my brother and sisters, and this little white girl kept on calling us niggers. My older sister Dottie was the one who finally said something.

She twisted around in her seat and said in a firm tone, "Please *do not* say that word again."

The girl narrowed her eyes, and her tiny mouth pulled up into a mean, little smirk.

"Niggers, niggers, *niggers,*" she repeated with glee.

My sister attempted a different strategy, turning back to face forward in her seat. Her face was tense, and she kept her mouth shut, but her chin grounded in a slow, circular motion.

The girl kept saying the word nigger, obviously taking a great deal of joy in harassing us, for what reason, I couldn't guess.

That day. I learned how ugly and hateful the word nigger really can be. The little girl knew hardly anything about us. So, why did she want to call us that ugly word and spread so much hate? Why did she have so much hate and anger in her heart? Who had taught her that such a terribly hurtful racial slur was okay to say?

My older sister ignored her as long as she could. There were only us and the little girl left on the bus before our stop. The rest of the kids lived inside of the city, while our two families lived further out, in the countryside that surrounded Fayetteville. I stared straight ahead, nestled in my bus seat in shock. I couldn't believe I was hearing the little girl still use that word.

    I thought the little girl would get sick of harassing us eventually, but after ten minutes she still hadn't stopped, and my older sister Dottie finally had enough. My sister spun around, without a word, and slapped the girl hard in the face. The girl's face snapped to the side, and the crack of my sister's palm striking her skin resounded through the bus. All was quiet for a moment, and then the little girl started to scream at the top of her lungs and cry profusely. As the bus driver pulled up to our house and as we got off the school bus, the little girl was still crying.

    The next day, both of our families had to go down to the school and talk to the principal. The girl's mother made the little girl apologize to us and promise to never use that word again. My mother had a long talk with her, saying that she'd always taught her children that all people are God's children regardless of their skin color. Hopefully, my mother taught the little girl a valuable life lesson that day.

    There were other times when Southern racism reared its ugly head in Fayetteville. I can recall the time my mother took my brother and sisters upon the town square, running some errands, and we came upon a large group of Ku Klux Klan holding a rally. My mother rushed us past them, fervently whispering, telling us not to look at them or start a conversation with them.

    Then there were also the so-called "friends" of my father, white men, who would come to the house and jokingly use that same horribly racist word. They would say the word "Nigger" without any shame, but they should have been ashamed to use such a word. I'll never understand why anyone would want to use a word which is used to insult a particular class of people. My parents taught me that God doesn't want us to tear people down; God wants all his children to build each other up, empower each other, and love one another.

Throughout all the good and bad times of my youth, I had my faith. I tried to pray for people with racism and hatred in their hearts. Faith was a huge part of our family upbringing, and I still lean on my faith today, going to God with all my troubles and triumphs. When I was a child, I made up a prayer that I still recite today.

"Thank you, Lord, for this great day.
I ask you, oh Lord, for another day.
I thank you for the good and the bad.
I ask you, oh Lord, to bless my family, friends, and enemies,
Forever and ever,
Amen."

I was going to need my faith and prayer the night I told my father about my plans to enlist in the Air Force. I knew he wasn't going to approve. Farming was everything to him, but it didn't hold the same meaning for me.

I wanted to leave behind my life of rural southern farming for other big adventures. I wanted to see and experience what the world had to offer me. I had big dreams and aspirations, and before I could set out to chase them, I had to break the news to my father that farming would not be in my future.

CHAPTER 2

Becoming Part Of Something Much Bigger

A great deal of my childhood was spent sneaking inside to watch *"American Band Stand, Soul Train,"* and other television favorite shows of mine during that era, and inevitably being chased back outside of the house by my father, to help with farm work. My father worked hard to build a life for himself and his family, and he wanted his children to be a part of what he'd built. Back then, I couldn't have cared less about farming. Nothing about it appealed to me, and I often found myself wishing that my father had a normal job outside of the house, one that he could keep regular hours with good pay.

Aside from watching Television, I loved going to school. From the very start of my education, I was very eager to learn. First and second grade was a bit of a challenge for me. I am so thankful to my first-grade teacher Mrs. Davidson for being so patient and understanding with me. Specifically, I remember in first grade being absolutely daunted by the letter "C." I would always write the letter C backward, no matter how hard I tried. Even if I were staring straight at the letter C, somehow, I would manage to write the letter backward.

Second and Third grade was a little better, but school still wasn't coming easily to me. It wasn't until fourth grade, everything started to fall into place. I'm not sure what happened, but all at once, everything clicked, and from then on, school was never the same struggle. All the basics that my first, second, and third-grade teachers had been pumping into my brain for the past few years were starting to fit together. The subjects in school made sense! Best of all, I could write every single one of the twenty-six letters of the alphabet correctly, even the previously dreaded C.

I loved Geography; I would challenge my sisters and brother to see who could name the most state capitals. Of course, I always won. I thought I was a genius. Math was my weakest subject, but somehow, I always passed the math test.

After school in the afternoons, my siblings and I were expected to help on the farm, as well as during the summer school break; we were expected to pitch in. The farm was our future, after all.

My family grew a few crops; corn and tobacco are two crops that I vividly remember. The corn sprouted before autumn. I remember the crisp sweetness of fresh corn with our suppers. The tobacco crops were lucrative. As the years went on, my father started a bush-hogging and bulldozering business and less of growing of crops. By the time I was in high school, my family's income had come primarily from bush-hogging and bulldozing for people in the local area.

For readers who do not know what a bush-hog is, it is a mowing device that hooks onto a tractor. It has a wide turning blade that is used to cut down high grass in large open areas, like fields or meadows. Most of our clients lived in the countryside and owned a lot of land with big fields and steep rolling hills. The people we bush-hogged for didn't have time to mow all those acres of land. They had regular jobs. The bush-hog and bulldozer business thrived in the spring and summer months. There were times when we'd have jobs scheduled every single day for weeks on end, with requests from both repeat customers and new ones alike. My father used the bulldozer to clean out ponds and clear land. He was also often hired for his bulldozering services when someone wanted to clear brush from land to build a new home or a business. The business was enough to provide for all of us to pay the family bills and business expenses. We had enough and what we needed. My parents instilled in all of us to work hard and be grateful for what we had.

I'd grown up knowing that my father expected me to help with the farm and business after high school graduation. As far as he was concerned, farming was in my DNA. I'd always felt that I was meant for something else, though. It was just before the end of my Senior year in high school when I got an inkling of what that something else might be.

I was sitting in the living room, watching television after a long day at school. I don't remember what I was watching, because it wasn't the television program that changed the course of my life; it was the commercial that came on the television. I was leaning back against the arm of the sofa, distractedly moving the remote from one hand to another, while I tried to decide whether to get up and start my homework or watch the rest of the show, when suddenly the screen of the small television set was filled with an inspirational call to action commercial. There was an airman in an Airforce Uniform with a deep voice spoke, as the commercial played, saying that your future could be with the United States Air Force. The Airman talked about the opportunities the Air Force would give someone interested in enlisting. And in a deep voice, the announcer said; "Aim High join the United States Airforce today!"

ABOUT FACE

A powerful wave of emotions and patriotism hit me. This was exactly the sort of inspiration and motivation I had been seeking. I knew it, right then and there, stronger than I'd ever known anything before; *this* was what I wanted to do with my life. I took note of the contact information that ended the commercial, explaining to the viewers how to get in contact with an Airforce Recruiter. I jumped up from the couch and hurried down the hall to my room to retrieve a pencil and paper. I quickly scribbled the phone number down before I had the chance to forget it.

I held a scrap of paper in my hand, pacing thoughtfully, back and forth across my room, thinking could I really have what it takes to enlist in the Air Force? Could I do something *that major?*

I thought on it long and hard. I thought about the television commercial for the rest of that night, and then the following night, and the following as well. It was an idea that I couldn't get out of my head. Enlisting in the Air force felt right, and I prayed about it. I thought about everything that enlisting in the Airforce would mean for my family and me. It would mean me completely stepping out of my comfort zone; it would mean brutal physical training. I wasn't out of shape, but if I wanted to make it as a member of any of the armed forces, I'd have to get into better shape. It would take hard work, an open mind, dedication, determination, and sticking with it when things got tough. Did I really want to go through all of that? Was I meant to enlist in the Airforce?

After a long week of rumination and careful thought, I realized what the answer was. It was a resounding *yes*. I knew what I needed to do. There was no need to be indecisive anymore. I had made my decision. Military life was in my future plans.

One day after school, when there was no one in the house, I picked up the telephone and contacted the Airforce Recruiter in my area.

CHAPTER 3

My Big Decision Point

The Air Force recruiter was very kind and attentive. I told him I was nearing graduation from high school, and I desired to enlist in the Air Force. We had a great conversation. The recruiter sounded upbeat and told me he'd like to meet with me. He told me all about the benefits of enlisting in the Air Force and how him becoming an airman had changed his life. He also explained the process of enlisting and provided me more information about the next steps needed to start the enlistment process.

After talking to the recruiter that day on the telephone, my decision was only solidified further. I was going to enlist in the Airforce. High school graduation was approaching. I knew it was time to talk to my parents about the decision I made. I couldn't let another day go by without telling them my plans after graduation. In my mind, I had already known what my father's reaction would be. His answer would be a resounding *no*. But I knew if I could get my mother's approval before talking to my father, my chances of convincing him of my decision would be much greater. So, I decided that after I completed my homework for the next day of class, I would talk to my mother before telling my father about my plans to enlist in the Airforce.

That same evening, I found my mother in the kitchen preparing dinner and told her I needed to talk with her. My face must have reflected my nerves because she stopped what she was doing, washing vegetables in the kitchen sink, turned the water off, and gave me an appraising look. Her eyebrows crinkled slightly, coming together at the bridge of her nose. She wiped her hands on a blue kitchen towel.

"Everything okay, Tom?" she asked. My family always calls me Tom. I knew I could talk to my mother about anything. Yes! I am a mama's boy.

"I want to talk to you about my plans after high school. I have an idea of what I'd like to do." I want to enlist in the Airforce".

She nodded and walked over to the kitchen table. I sat down across from her and laid out my plans. I explained what enlisting in the Air Force meant to me. I told her how I'd seen the commercial on television, spent some time thinking it over, and ultimately decided to call the local area Airforce Recruiter.

I ended my lengthy confession by saying, "And so that's what I did today. The recruiter thought I was a great candidate to enlist. I really want to get started with everything."

She nodded, lightly tapping her finger under her chin.

"I think it's a good idea," she said, after a long moment of thought. "It could be good for your future. Could open a lot of doors for you."

"You're okay with this then?"

"At the end of the day you are now a grown man, it isn't my decision, Tom. It's yours, and I'll support whatever decision you make. You must do what feels right to you. It's your life."

I grinned.

"Thanks, Mom. That means a lot to me."

She gave me a serious look, then.

"But you know your father isn't going to feel the same way," she said. "He wants you to join him in the family business after you graduate. I just want you to be prepared for his reaction. When are you going to tell him?"

I swallowed, fidgeting with an edge of the tablecloth.

"Tonight, at dinner."

She sighed.

"Don't be discouraged if he doesn't take it well," she murmured. "Keep your head up and tell him that you have already made your decision."

"I will."

In waiting for dinner and the conversation I knew that was going to take place, the hours crawled by like sickly slugs. I dreaded telling my father my plans. My mom was right. He wasn't going to take it well. I felt a twisting and hardening in my gut. My stomach tightened and convulsed, bringing my emotional state into the physical realm. I paced back and forth in my room, rehearsing what I would say to him. I worded and reworded, each time trying to be more persuasive. I thought that if I could come up with the exact right combination of words, then maybe he'd be on my side, perhaps he wouldn't feel like I was abandoning the family business after all.

My father came home just before five-thirty, and mom called all of us to dinner at six. With my hands clenched tightly at my sides, I made my way out to the dining table. I had planned to break the news to him as soon as grace had been said, but everyone started eating, I couldn't find the words. I took a bite, and then another, trying to think about how to start the conversation. Dinner went on, and my siblings chatted about their days at school, all the while, my mother kept giving me expectant looks, urging me to gather my courage and speak up. Eventually, I realized that everyone was nearly finished eating. I couldn't put this off a moment later. I convinced myself it was now or never.

"Dad," I said, with a shaking voice. "I need to talk to you about the decision I've made."

He lifted his eyes and set down his last spoonful of pinto beans on the edge of his plate.

"Alright, then."

I pulled at a thread hanging from the seam of my jeans. This was going to be awkward, but it was better to get it over and done with. I didn't want to drag this out. I took a deep breath, opened my mouth, and blurted it out.

"I know what I want to do after I graduate high school."

He made a move to interrupt me, starting to speak, but I kept going, talking louder. I had to get this off my chest.

"I'm going to enlist in the Air Force. I spoke to a recruiter yesterday. It's a good opportunity for me. I'll get to travel, learn a skill, go to college, and serve my country. I'm going to start the enlistment process soon. I must take a test and do a few other things. This is what I want to do with my life."

My father stared at me. His eyes were hard. For a long, drawn-out moment, he didn't say one word. Nobody did. My mother sat wordlessly but communicating to me all the same. She wore a soft smile, and gave me a discreet, approving head nod. My brother and sisters looked back and forth between father and me, waiting for one of us to speak.

Father did say something, and when he did, he absolutely exploded.

"I don't know what you think you're going on about, but you aren't doing any such thing. Now you stop talking that Airforce stuff around me. Your place is here on the farm, with the rest of us!"

"But Dad, that isn't what I want"

"Who asked you what you want? Drop it. You aren't too good for the family farm."

"Dad, listen!"

"No, *you* listen!" he snapped. "When you graduate, your place is here to work with us on the farm. Do you hear me? Now, that is final!"

"Enough!"

My mother's voice, from out of nowhere grew louder than my father's. Her voice somehow made my father very silent. He gritted his teeth together and gave her a stony look.

"Tom is about to be grown," she continued in a firm voice. "It isn't your place to tell him what to do anymore. It is his life; It's what he decides to make."

Father looked away. His face was tight.

"We can't make his choice for him, all we can do is love and support him; that's all any loving parents can do for their grown children."

My siblings left the table, and my parents and I kept talking for a good long time. My father wasn't happy, but in the end, he said that he accepted my decision, I was glad to have my mother's support.

I went to bed that night feeling a torrential storm of different emotions. I was relieved that the conversation was over. I was saddened that my father had been so angry and disappointed in me. I hoped that he would get past his initial reactions, and eventually, he did.

The very last emotion to surface in my heart, just as I was laying my head on my pillow and saying my nightly prayer, was incredible anxiety. Now it was time to take the next step. I was about to start the Airforce enlistment process. I knew my life was about to change forever.

CHAPTER 4

High School Graduation And My Misfortune

At the high school graduation ceremony, I received my diploma along with a certificate for twelve years of perfect attendance. Yep! Not one day missed in school for twelve years. When I tell people that story these days, they call me a school nerd. It was a great feeling to hear that the master of ceremonies announce my perfect attendance to the applauding crowd attending the graduation ceremony, as I walked across the stage to receive my high school diploma. This was a major accomplishment for me.

Within two weeks after high school graduation, I met with the recruiter to schedule a date to take the Armed Services Vocational Aptitude Battery (ASVAB) test. The ASVAB is a multiple choice test used to determine qualifications in the United States Armed Forces. I studied a lot in preparation for the ASVAB test. I'd never been good at taking tests. The ASVAB test was lengthy and somewhat intimidating. I tried my best on every single question. But I was only allowed to spend a certain amount of time on each of the nine sections of the test.

I knew if I didn't get a high enough score, I'd have to pass up my dream of joining the Air Force or re-take the test until I passed it. I didn't know what I'd do with myself if that occurred. I had no fallback plan. Most of my friends were going off to college in the fall, but I couldn't do that. My family didn't have the money for college tuition.

After taking the ASVAB test, I waited restlessly to hear back about my scores. Weeks passed without hearing anything. I tried to distract myself by, helping with the bush-hogging (it was the busy season, after all) and watching television. All I could do was wait. There were times when I'd restlessly flip through the pamphlets the recruiter had given me, staring at the pictures and reading the content, hoping beyond hope that my dream wasn't going to slip right past me.

When almost a month had gone by without any news, I gave the recruiter a call. He wasn't available, and I had to leave a message. After a few days, I tried calling again. I left another message.

"Have some patience," my mother urged. "I'm sure everything will be fine. You did your part. It's in their hands now. Say a prayer and hold tight."

I held tight.

Finally, near the end of that week, the recruiter returned my call.

My mother whispered to me that the Air Force recruiter was on the telephone. I took the phone from her with my hands shaking.

I cleared my throat.

"Hello, this is Thomas."

"Good afternoon, Thomas. I'm calling to talk about your ASVAB test results."

"Yes, are my scores high enough to enlist in the Airforce I asked?"

There was a pause.

"No, Thomas. I'm afraid your scores weren't high enough."

My heart dropped to my feet. In that instant, it was like my soul had bottomed out.

"We won't be able to move forward with the enlistment process until you obtain high enough scores on the ASVAB," he continued. "I'm sorry for the disappointing news."

In a devastated and shaky voice, I told him that I understood and thanked him for calling me back. I hung up the telephone and just sat there and stared into the deep space for a moment regarding my misfortune.

My mother had been standing outside the kitchen, listening to the conversation. She must have been able to guess what the conversation had entailed from the defeated look on my face. She approached me with a cautious smile, placing a hand lightly on my arm.

"It will all work out, Tom," she said softly. "You'll figure something else out maybe you just have to retake the test again."

I nodded numbly. I couldn't believe that I did not do well on the test. I had been worried about this exact circumstance, but now that it was a reality, I felt thrown by it.

I spent the following days trying to decide what my next steps would be. I helped my father and brother on the farm, trying to figure out if bush-hogging and farming was something that I could do for the rest of my life. It didn't feel like the right path for me, but at the same time, I didn't think there were other options available for me. If I couldn't enlist in the Airforce, then working on the family farm was the only thing left that made sense.

Two days after that first telephone call, the telephone rang again. It was the recruiter, and he said that he had some good news for me.

"Great," I said, twisting the beige telephone cord around my fingers.

"So, I took another look at your scores."

My heart began to patter in my chest. Was it possible? Was I getting a second chance?

"As you know your scores weren't high enough to enlist in the Air Force…"

I could feel my chest constrict.

"But they are high enough to enlist in the Army. Is that something you'd be interested in?"

Excitement filled me. This wasn't a path that I'd considered, but now I was being offered another window of opportunity, I was filled with a mixture of questions and excitement.

"I'm not sure," I answered honestly. "I think that it could be."

"Well, I work with a lot of army recruiters. I'd be happy to get you in touch with someone who could give you more information."

"Thank you so much for the opportunity," I said. "And I think I might like to take you up on that offer, but I have to talk to my mom about it before I commit to anything. She supported me enlisting in the Air Force, so I need to see how she feels about me enlisting in the Army."

"Understandable, Thomas. Talk to your mother, tell her you've still got the chance to serve your country and see the world in the Army. See what she has to say about it, and if you both agree that you want to know more, give me a call back."

"Thank you for calling. I'll be in touch very soon."

I hung up the telephone phone, feeling absolutely invigorated. I rushed right out to the living room and relayed to my mother the conversation that had taken place. She was happy and supportive of me. She said she was glad I'd still be able to enlist in the Army.

I called the recruiter back the next day and told him I'd decided I would like to know more about enlisting in the Army. He said that he'd put me in touch with an Army recruiter and explained I should expect a telephone call soon. Three days later, I received a telephone call from the Army recruiter, and we scheduled a time for him to come over the house the following week.

As scheduled, the recruiter came to the house. We sat down at the kitchen table, and he explained to me my scores were high enough to enlist in the army. We talked in-depth about what enlisting in the Army would mean for my life, briefly what basic training would entail. When he was done explaining all the specifics, he said that if I was sure I wanted to enlist, then all I had to do was sign some paperwork today to start the enlistment process.

"If we start the process now, then you could leave for basic training at the end of September."

Basic training is also commonly called Recruit Training or boot camp. Basic training prepares recruits for all elements of service: physical, mental, and emotional throughout their military tours.

"September, I asked|?"

"Yes, the end of September the recruiter said again." But that was so soon! It was hardly more than a month away. Could I really leave it all behind so quickly?

I waffled with indecision for a moment, and then I made my decision.

"I'll sign the papers now," I said. "I know this is what I want to do."

He handed me a silver pen, and I signed my name with a flourish. This was the beginning of something which seemed so surreal.

That night I laid in bed, wondering if I'd done the right thing. Did I make the right decision? After tossing, turning, ruminating at length and praying again, the answer was *yes*. This was the path that I was meant to be on, and while part of me was rattled with nerves, another part of me was reverberating with excitement. I was going to get travel. I'd never been out of Tennessee, and I wanted to experience all that the world had to show and offer me. I'd make a better life for myself and my family. I'd earn steady income in the Army and get to send money back to help with the farm. I could even get to attend college in my spare time once I arrive at my permanent duty station. As a Soldier, the Army would pay me a salary and plus pay for my college, sweet deal!

Weeks later, the recruiter took me to the Nashville Military Entrance Processing Station (MEPS) to receive the military entrance physical exam. If you pass your physical, you are sworn in to the military the next day. This required an overnight stay in Nashville. It was my first time ever sleeping in a hotel and being away from home. Throughout it all, I was painstakingly excited, but also nervous. I passed my physical exam and was sworn in the next day, beginning my three-year enlistment in the Army. It was official I could now be called Private (E1) Taylor. I would leave for basic training on September 30, 1981.

The rest of the days of summer flew by in a blur of barely solid colors and sounds. I was so filled with emotions and anxiousness. I kept myself busy trying to prepare myself for basic training. I read anything; I picked up books at the library and read them.

The day came, arriving much sooner than I'd ever anticipated, to leave for basic training. One day it was mid-August, and then, all at once, time seemed to speed up, moving at a breakneck pace. On a warm September fall morning, my mom and two sisters drove me to the Nashville Airport to see me off to basic training. My father and brother couldn't be there, as the family business was still too busy for them to get away. I'd said my good-byes to them the night before. I hugged my mom and sisters, told them I'd miss them, and boarded an airplane for the very first time in my life. I felt excited. I was off to go be a Soldier in the Army.

CHAPTER 5

Embrace The Suck; You're In The Army Now!

I settled back in my seat as the airplane ascended into the clouds. The Capitan from the cockpit came over the intercom and announced,
"I would like to welcome you all aboard the flight."
"The cruising altitude will be thirty-five thousand feet, folks just sit back, relax, and enjoy the flight into Saint Louis."
As the white puffy clouds rolled by, I knew there was no turning back. I didn't have any regrets about leaving Fayetteville, but it was still going to be tough to get used to living away from home, away from my family and everything I'd ever known most my childhood. Basic Training was going to be a huge adjustment for me. I'd signed on the dotted line as we say in the Army, for a three-year enlistment. During the flight, I thought of my mother and how she'd supported my decision. I knew I would be forever grateful to her for standing by me. I remember my mom giving me a big red delicious apple for good luck before I boarded the airplane in Nashville. I guess my luck ran out after I ate that red apple during the flight.
My arrival at the Saint Louis Airport didn't get off to a good start. The airplane landed, and all passengers were instructed to pick up their luggage at one of the baggage carousels in the airport. I stood patiently waiting for what seemed like a very long time, but my luggage never arrived. I wasn't sure what to do.

When the Non-Commissioned Officer(NCO) came to meet the new recruits to escort us to the holding area, I nervously followed along behind him. I wanted to speak up about my lost luggage but was too tongue-tied. Another sergeant came in, greeting the group of recruits and issuing instructions. We were escorted to a bus idling in the airport arrival parking area. The bus transported us to the Battalion Reception Station located on the Fort Leonard Wood Army Base. It wasn't until we arrived at the reception station, I found my voice and talked to the reception drill sergeant who greeted us, that my luggage never arrived off the airplane at the airport and I didn't know what to do about it. He was very kind, telling me he would have the reception personnel contact the airport to see if they could locate my luggage. Spoiler alert: the airport never found my luggage. I had to adjust my first couple of days away from home without even a pair of fresh socks or a change of underwear.

The sergeant must have known this was upsetting to me. I distinctly remember him reassuring me I wouldn't need any civilian clothes in Basic Training, and that the Army would provide me with all that I needed.

"You belong to the Army now," he said with a genuine smile. "Uncle Sam won't let you go without."

He was right about that, and the welcome gifts started almost right away. The next couple of days were a blur of activity. There was more paperwork to be signed and processed. I received shots. Each recruit was issued five Olive-Green Shade Army and two Army Dress Green Uniforms along with accessories. Later in my training, all recruits got issued the Woodland Camouflage Battle Dress Uniform. Last, but not least, I was given that stylish haircut that all new recruits are familiar with. I sat stock-still in the chair, as the barber's clippers buzzed my full head of hair in like ten seconds.

Throughout, the reception personnel and drill sergeants were very nice. A bit too nice, I thought. For the first few days, they were helpful and friendly, explaining everything that was going to happen in the next couple of weeks. I knew this kind of treatment couldn't last long. In a lot of ways, we were still acting a lot like civilians. We weren't living out regimented schedules yet. We got three meals a day at the dining facility and were still able to consume the meals in a somewhat relaxed environment.

It was once we left the Battalion Reception Station and arrived at Echo Company, reality finally set in. There was a marked difference in the way the drill sergeants treated us. They were no longer welcoming and helpful. Instead, all the words out of their mouth, directing us were loud and harsh. It was a lot of yelling, screaming, and chaos ordering us to get off the bus and get into a push-up position.

"Welcome to Hell Week, you dirt bags," the drill sergeants screamed! "You need to learn to embrace the suck; you're in the Army now!" one of the drill sergeants shouted.

From then on, we had no more freedoms. We had to be broken down so that the Army could build us back up and transform us from civilians to Army Soldiers. The drill sergeants had total control over us now. We slept, ate, and breathed when they said to. We spent a lot of time range walking, sometimes running, all while getting shouted at to run faster, jump higher, and show what we were really made of.

There were times during that first week of basic training, I felt I was not going to make it. My body was continually put through pure hell. My spirit and confidence were pushed to the limits. I wondered if I'd ever live up to the drill sergeant's expectations. What would happen to me if I didn't have the physical strength and mental toughness it took to be in the Army? At night in the dining facility, tired and covered in mud and grime, I pulled together every ounce of strength and optimism in my heart and willed myself to keep going. There was one thing that I knew for sure; I *did* want it enough, and I was no quitter.

Week one was a true test for a shy and introverted country boy from Tennessee. I was pushed to my limits, both physically, mentally, and emotionally. I missed my family and all the familiar comforts of home. There was so much to get used to in this new army life. One of the greatest shocks to me was the total and complete lack of privacy. I slept, ate, and lived twenty-four-seven around other recruits. We lived in open bay barracks and shared communal showers for personal hygiene. There wasn't one moment when I was free to be alone with my thoughts. I have to admit the communal showers was tough for me to get accustomed to.

Every morning at four-thirty, we were awakened by the charge of quarters sergeant to get ready for morning Physical Training(PT) exercise in rain, sleet, and cold Missouri weather. After PT, we were released from formation to take a five-minute shit, shower, and shave. Then, it was time to march to the dining facility for breakfast. We had only twenty minutes to scarf down breakfast and then go back through the serving line to grab a packaged Meal Ready to Eat (MRE) for our lunch meal. Mealtimes were not a time to socialize and was serious business. While eating, we couldn't talk or look at any of the other recruits. It was time to put fuel in our bodies, fuel that we would desperately need to finish out the rest of the grueling training day.

Let's not forget the long marches in formations to the weapons and training ranges, all while screaming Army cadences at the top of our lungs in perfect unison. Sometimes we would take the old cattle cars due to inclement weather.

I lost count of how many push-ups I did. It had to be in the thousands. If we went anywhere, we went by running or range-walking. It was never a relaxed stroll. Nothing was relaxing about Basic Training. Boot camp pushed me harder than I'd ever been pushed before.

CHAPTER 6

That Good Ole Army Training: Drill Sergeant!

During basic training, you form strong bonds with other recruits. It only took a few days in the barracks before all the recruits were comfortable with each other and started to function as a team.

Through all the struggles and obstacles, we faced as a company, we helped each other through them. We became like a band of brothers. Echo company was made up of a bunch of dysfunctional recruits from all different races, religions, upbringings, and political ideologies. As a unit, we did a lot of idiotic things together. During downtime some nights, I can remember all of us laughing together in the barracks mocking the drill sergeants' catchphrases they yelled at us for that day. One of the phrases the drill sergeants would ask us daily,

"What type of training you want Privates today?"

We would reply in unison at the top of our lungs,

"We want that good ole army training drill sergeant!"

And that's exactly what the drill sergeants provided us. After a long day of training in the cold weather, pouring rain or whatever else mother nature had in store for us, in the barracks, we would laugh ourselves silly over the most ridiculous stuff that happened that day. It was our way of unwinding and letting go of the days training stressors.

We were all there for each other, no matter what; when I was homesick, when I didn't think I'd make it through the day's training or when I didn't qualify with my weapon the first time around, it was the other recruits who lifted me up, giving me the encouragement I needed to keep going. They reminded me that each person here was struggling with something. Boot Camp wasn't meant to be easy. If it were easy, everybody would be doing it.

I was glad Echo Company was starting to build unit team cohesion. Especially, when it was time for Gas Chamber Training, and if that sounds terrifying to you, let me confirm; it absolutely *was*. It was during the second month of Basic Training that the gas chamber training took place. The unit marched out to the gas chamber early one fall morning. I was anxious but glad to have my new brothers by my side. I wasn't going through the gas chamber training alone.

We were scheduled to go through the gas chamber in the afternoon. The drill sergeants suggested to us earlier in the day, we should eat light and refrain from drinking a lot of water from our canteens. When you are going through the gas chamber, the chances of vomiting were extremely high due to the smell of the CS gas. I'd barely eaten any breakfast or consumed my MRE that day. My stomach still felt queasy. Before the training began, I stood with the rest of the recruits, listening raptly as the drill sergeant explained how the gas chamber training would work.

We would be broken up into smaller groups, and we'd enter the chamber in clusters of five to ten Soldiers. We would remain in the chamber for somewhere between three to five minutes. How long we remained inside would depend on how well we tolerated the gas. We were each issued a gas mask and chemical protective gear. We spent several minutes going over how to fit the mask on our faces, and how to properly wear the chemical gear. I listened carefully to these instructions, but I noticed that some of the other recruits in my platoon weren't paying attention. I shook my head. I figured they were probably going to end up regretting letting their attention wander later.

"Now, here's how this is going to work," the drill sergeant barked. "You'll line up outside the chamber and put your gear on. Then you'll enter the chamber, where you'll be met by the sergeant. The chamber will already be filled with gas. When the sergeant taps you on the shoulder, you are to lift your gas mask, state your rank, name, and your social security number. You can try not to breathe the gas, but it probably won't do you much good. The point of this exercise is to get a whiff of the gas. If you know how it feels to take a lungful of CS Gas, then you'll have proper respect for your gear, and you'll sure as heck remember how to use it said the sergeant."

And with that terrifying explanation, we were sorted into groups. I was with a group of about five other recruits. We lined up outside of the chamber and fitted the gas masks to our faces. I must have checked and double-checked my mask thirty times in ten minutes as we stood waiting our turn to enter the gas chamber.

Before I knew it, it was my group's turn to enter the chamber. With bated breath, I followed the rest of my group, as we were ushered into the chamber. Even with my eyes closed, they were burning. I told myself that I could do this. I'd already been through so much. This was just one more step on my journey to graduate basic training and become a real Soldier. I could do it. I *had* to do it.

I stood and waited for my turn to be tapped on the shoulder by the sergeant. I dreaded removing my gas mask. Even with the gas mask over my mouth and nose, I could smell the rancid CS gas burning. It seeped through the military-grade protective mask. I steeled myself for the worst. This was not going to be fun.

I stood stiffly, keeping my eyelids shut tight.

I felt a tap on my shoulder. The drill sergeant was waiting for me to lift my mask and speak. I raised a hand to do that, and suddenly, an extreme panic overtook me. What were my rank and name? Or my social security number for that matter? I was so flooded with anxiety that for a fleeting second, I couldn't recall even the simplest of information.

Thankfully, that moment passed. I reminded myself that I could do this. I had to do this because the longer I took, the longer my battle buddies had to stand in the gas chamber breathing in this scalding gas. I took a deep breath, lifted my mask, and in one great burst, shouted out all the information. Then I shoved the mask back onto my face. I had done it. I'd made it through.

As we left the gas chamber, my eyes were pouring water, and mucus was flowing out of my nose. My entire face was burning from the CS gas. Stepping out into the sunlight, I hastily removed the gas mask, coughing, and spluttering. I took in great gasping breaths of fresh air. Some of my battle buddies, as I'd expected, were in far worse shape than I was. They hadn't paid attention well enough to properly fit their masks to their faces, and as a result, had inhaled quite a bit more of the CS gas than I had. There was a good deal of retching, and recruits doubled-over clutching their knees when they exited the gas chamber.

We all got through it in the end, though. We'd been told to open our eyes immediately after exiting the chamber. I did this straight away, and as we pulled off our protective gear, the drill sergeants were there shouting at us not to touch our eyes. We were reminded to take deep breaths, with our arms held up high over our heads and now to drink lots of water from our canteens. It amazed me how quickly the effects of the CS gas dissipated. It only took a couple of minutes for me to get back to feeling normal.

Other than the obstacles courses, the Gas Chamber was one of the toughest challenges of Basic Training, but who am I kidding? All of basic training was tough. Basic Training makes you stronger, tougher, more resilient, and about thirty pounds lighter, not to mention in much better shape. Basic Training hardened me mentally, physically, and emotionally, preparing me for the tours ahead in my military career.

I had thought I'd known what to expect when I'd enlisted, but there's really no way to know what you're in for until you experience it. Basic training is its own unique world. It's like the infamous phrase, "You think you know, but you have *no* idea!" That was the truth. When I'd first gotten off that airplane, I'd had no idea what to expect. None of recruits did. As boot camp was coming to an end, I felt proud of myself and what I was about to accomplish.

We were being transformed from civilians to recruits to Soldiers during the ten weeks of basic training. I spent a lot of time cursing the extreme cold temperatures of Missouri and the drill sergeants under my breath, of course. Being challenged, building your character, and molding you into a Soldier is what basic training will do. I hated it then. But, now that I look back and reminisce, basic training was the best thing that happened to me at such a young age.

For those of you readers who are getting ready to leave for basic training, allow me to take a moment to give you some encouragement. If I can provide a piece of advice, it is this: There might be times when you want to give up, times when the burden feels too heavy, and you question if you made the right choice to enlist in the Army. I had those moments too. You must keep going, keep working, keep pushing yourself, lean on the other recruits for strength and encouragement when you find it lacking in yourself. Don't give up! Embrace the suck!

CHAPTER 7

Not My Soda Can Drill Sergeant!

During basic training, there were many fights among the recruits in the barracks. I saw tears that sprung forth among some of the toughest recruits who received those "Dear John" letters from their girlfriends back home. But, most of all, there was "Esprit de corps" in the company. No matter what was thrown our way, we vowed to make it to graduation day as a company.

There was always recruits who challenged some of the strict rules enforced by the drill sergeants in the barracks. I think that is what caused most of the fights. When rules were broken, all recruits would pay the price. For example, we were not allowed to have any food or drinks, commonly called contraband, in the barracks after certain hours. The drill sergeants would routinely conduct a nightly walk through the barracks, just before lights out to ensure none of us sneaked contraband items in the barracks.

One night during a final walk-through, the drill sergeant found a soda can in the barracks area. The drill sergeant walked into our living area with an angered look on his face and held up the soda can. It sure wasn't going to be a pretty sight that night nor, an easy training day the next morning.

"Recruits, on your feet and stand at parade rest!" He belted out.

"Who does this soda can belong to?" he shouted.

None of us recruits said anything.

I kept my arms at parade rest, standing at the end of my cot, perfectly in line with all my other platoon buddies. There was dead silence in the barracks.

"I asked who does this belongs to!" The drill sergeant yelled, even louder now. "Is someone going to confess? Or, are all of you going to pay the price for not following my rules."

Not one single recruit uttered a word.

The drill sergeant went ballistic. He yelled, screamed, kicked trashcans, getting up in faces of select recruits who the drill sergeant assumed the soda can belong to. These recruits already had caused trouble in the company throughout basic training.

"Not my soda can", shouted one of the recruits to the drill sergeant."

In the end, we all had to pay for whoever had broken the no food and soda rule. The drill sergeant ordered all of us to get into the push-up position until someone confessed.

Pressing our palms into the hard cold and dirty barracks floor, keeping our bodies stiff as planks, waiting for someone to confess. Still, no one owned up to it. So, the drill sergeant passed the soda can around to each recruit and made us all take a sip from the soda can, moving from one hand to the next, and all the while, the drill sergeant kept on demanding that someone confess. I can still remember the slimy taste of all the other recruits accrued spit on the rim of the soda can as I got my turn to take a sip. That night was pure hell. I think we got roughly two hours of sleep before morning wake-up call.

As boot camp was coming to an end, graduation was almost upon us. I was proud of the other recruits who stuck it out for the grueling ten-weeks of basic training. Some recruits did not make it through due to getting injured during training exercises. The injured recruits were recycled or held over for the next basic training class. Some recruits just gave up and were discharged. I was not a quitter. My goal was to graduate basic training and make a career in the army.

Before graduation, there was a vast field training exercise. The field training exercise was surprisingly fun. A few days after the field training exercise, a graduation ceremony was held. We were sharply dressed in our army dress uniforms, our heads held high and this time gleefully singing army cadences in unison as we proudly marched onto the parade field for the start of the ceremony.

Many of the recruit's families attended the ceremony. The graduation marked the transition from being called an Army Recruit for the last ten weeks, to now officially being called an Army Soldier. I was prouder than I'd ever been since receiving that applause from the crowd during my high school graduation and achieving the twelve years of perfect attendance honor. Later that day, we received telephone privileges. I called my family and told them I graduated basic training. My family was so proud of me and my accomplishment. They could not wait until I came home on leave to visit them. I know each trial, tribulation, and push up was well worth it during basic training. I can truly say thank you to all the Soldiers who were assigned to Echo Company for being there for me. Thank you drill sergeants. You gave us all hell! Oh, and by the way, not my soda can drill seargeant!

CHAPTER 8

Germany, Here I Come

The next eight-weeks of training was the Advanced Individual Training (AIT). I was assigned to S Company/ 4th Training Battalion at Fort Lee, Virginia. This phase of training is when a Soldier is trained in a specific skill, they'll use for their Military Occupational Specialty (MOS). A Soldier's MOS is basically the job that they will be performing while serving in the Army. My assigned MOS was 76Y (Unit Supply Specialist).

I adjusted quickly to the second phase of training. AIT training was a little different than basic training. The training atmosphere was a little more relaxed, no drill sergeants to scream at you every hour, or on the hour. Over time, the company gradually earned more privileges to go to the Post Exchange(PX). A post exchange is basically like Walmart but on an army base. We were able to earn more freedom with hard work in class and good behavior. I put everything I had into learning the skills I'd need to ensure I was prepared for my first duty station assignment.

Just before graduating from the last phase of AIT training, I discovered my first duty station would be overseas. My orders read: "You are ordered to the 32nd Army Air Defense Command in Schweinfurt, Germany as a unit supply specialist." I was thrilled and filled with nerves all at the same time. I knew very little about Germany except studying about the country in my geography class in high school. I certainly was not familiar with the language. I had a lot of preparation ahead of me.

Thankfully, after graduation from AIT, I was granted thirty days of military leave to spend at home with my family before leaving for Germany. I recall my greyhound bus ticket getting cancelled that night. So, I took a taxicab from Fort Lee, Virginia, to Fayetteville. When I arrived home with my two Army duffel bags in hand, my mother and siblings greeted me at the front door. My mother pulled me into her arms. I hugged her back tightly. I'd missed my family more than words could say for the last eighteen-weeks.

When my father met me at the house, coming inside from a long day of working on the family farm, he gave me an appraising look, and then pulled me in for a quick hug, patting me brusquely on the back.

"It's good to see you, Tom. Looks like they really whipped you into shape."

He didn't say it, but I could tell he was proud of me. The words didn't need to be spoken. Knowing there were good feelings between us again was enough for me.

I spent the next four weeks, resting and recuperating, catching up with my family, catching up on all the city gossip in Fayetteville, and learning everything that I could about Germany. I tried to teach myself the German language. I struggled, and my mother told me not to worry.

"I'm sure you'll start to pick up the language, and the army will make sure you get the language training you need really quickly once you're actually over there," she reassured me.

My siblings were just as supportive and excited for me. When I was feeling especially nervous about living in Germany, my older sister talked me down, reminding me that I was going to get to travel to the world. Just like I wanted to.

"You're going to see a whole new country," she told me. "That's an opportunity a lot of people would love to have. Enjoy it. You're going to learn so much and see so much."

I took my families words to heart. I knew they were right. At the same time, it was hard not to feel apprehensive. Basic and AIT Training had been a tough adjustment, but this next move was to a whole other continent. I worried I wasn't ready, that I wouldn't cope well with all the changes. Still, while home on leave, I prepared with every spare moment. I visited old friends. I spent time enjoying the days with my family and enjoying the town I had missed for some many weeks. It felt good to be back home for a while.

The month flew by, and I was back at the Nashville Airport before I knew what was happening. Once again, I hugged my family goodbye and boarded a plane bound to Atlanta, Hartsfield- Jackson Airport. My siblings told me they would miss me and asked me to write often. I promised them I would, and I boarded a airplane for the third time in my life.

It was a short forty-five-minute flight from Nashville to Atlanta before the dreaded long flight to Frankfurt, Germany. During the flight to Germany, I tried to occupy myself by reading books I'd brought along for the flight. I talked to other Soldiers on the airplane who was going to be a station in Germany. I'd never flown across the Atlantic Ocean before. Looking out the airplane window over the ocean was such a beautiful sight to see. I saw nothing but large masses of water. I must admit I was riddled with nerves and excited at the same time.

By the time the airplane landed at the Frankfort Airport in Germany, I was exhausted. I hadn't been able to sleep very much during the flight. I walked through the airport with fear zipping through my veins. Also, ahead of me was an hour and a half bus ride to the Schweinfurt, Germany Army Base. I spent my first couple of days in Germany feeling like I'd been hit by a bus. I was tired, weak, and had a headache that wouldn't go away. Other Soldiers on the flight with me explained that I was just jet-lagged. They told me to push through the headache, and that it would go away soon. They were right. By the end of the week, I felt much better.

I was so far out of my depth. I didn't know how I was going to make my way in a country where I wouldn't even be able to communicate with a good deal of people. I felt a little bit out of my comfort zone again. My assignment in Germany would be fifteen-months long. That was fifteen-months in a brand-new country, one with a language barrier, new customs, and social norms drastically different from the ones I'd been accustomed to in the states.

I spent two weeks at Ledward/Conn Barracks in Schweinfurt, Germany, before being released to my assigned unit. It was a requirement for all new Soldiers to attend a two-week German language training course to improve our language skills and learn some of the basic cultural etiquettes in the country. My mother was right. The army took care of me again and provided me the tools needed to ensure I was successful in Germany. To pass the class, there were a few keywords and phrases that I had to learn. These included: "Hallo" (Hello), "Guten Morgen" (Good Morning), "Auf Wiedersehen" (Goodbye), "Danke" (Thank You), and lastly, "Wie viel kostet das?" (How much does this cost?).

I was glad language training had been mandatory. Knowing some of the most important words and key phrases made interacting with the locals much easier.

Despite the challenges, I adjusted to life in Germany and received my first promotion to the private second class. It was a long way from Fayetteville, Tennessee and I had to motivate myself to make the best of the situation in Germany. Living conditions had improved from basic training and AIT. The rooms in the barracks accommodated three Soldiers. We still had to share a communal shower but only with the three Soldiers assigned to the room. Making friends with other Soldiers helped me through my overseas assignment. There were two Soldiers I met. They were Private Second-Class Darren Jackson and Private Second-Class David Talarczyk.

After we'd all settled into the swing of daily life in Germany, PV2 Jackson, PV2 Talarczyk and I started running and working out at the gym together. It became a regular part of our daily routine. During time off, we went into the city, site seeing. On several occasions, when we were granted an off-duty four-day pass, we would go on tours to other cities in Germany. We all agreed while we were in the country, we should take full advantage of making the most of it. After all, leadership did not want us to become "barracks rats."

The days turned into weeks, turned into months, and I slowly became acclimated to my new life and surroundings. I had made great friends; I loved my job working as a unit supply specialist in the company. I was learning so much every day about how the army really worked. I was experiencing a brand-new country, seeing the world, and growing stronger physically and mentally.

About a year into my assignment, my life in Germany took a turn for the worse. I was about to experience a dark moment in my life and military career. Nothing could prepare me for it. My dignity and sense of self-worth would be violently stolen from me one night. A moment I would have to live with for the rest of my life.

CHAPTER 9

The Darkest Day Of My Life

It was one of those dreary nights that makes it feel much later and darker than it is. I sat on the edge of my bed, reading through some of the letters from my family I had received from the early morning mail call that day.

I finished reading the letters and set them down on the table beside me with a yawn. I stretched my arms out in front of me. The afternoon's workout, along with the morning physical training (PT), had been particularly rigorous, and I was feeling tired.

I was the only one in the room at the barracks. The other Soldiers had gone out for the night. I can't remember where it was, they had gone that night. It's the details of what happened *after* they left that stick in my mind.

I was trying to decide whether to find a book to read or listen to my favorite music on my Walkman, before going to bed for the night, when I heard a set of footsteps entering my room. My head snapped up. Another Soldier came into the room. Normally, this wouldn't strike me as odd, but I did not recognize the Soldier as one of my two roommates. It was also the look on the Soldiers face that alarmed me. The Soldier was deadly serious, with eyes fixed on me like daggers, something unidentifiable rising in them.

I didn't say anything to him. I didn't have the chance, not before he was on me. He clamped his hands around my throat, crushing my windpipe and held the blade of a knife to my throat.

"I'll kill you if you don't do what I say," he said with a high-pitched voice.

I could smell his sour breath. I closed my eyes, wondering what I should do, hoping that my roommates would come back an rescue me before this Soldier had a chance to enact whatever nefarious plans he had.

He continued to whisper angrily into my ear. He told me that if I did not become aroused, he would kill me.

That's when I knew what he was going to do to me. I tried to brace myself for it, but there isn't any way to brace for something like that.

He pushed me down, climbed atop me, and raped me. There is no other way I can say. He raped me!

I felt myself go numb. I detached from myself. I could feel every thrust. I could feel his weight on me, his skin on my skin. It didn't feel like it was really me that this was happening to. It was like I was watching it happen to another version of me.

He kept on raping me. It felt like it went on forever. He raped me until he achieved orgasm.

When he was finished, he held the knife against my throat and threatened me repeatedly.

"If you tell anyone about this, I will kill you."

I nodded, tears trailing down my face.

He left.

I watched him leave, I fell into a shaking, sobbing, and emotional numbness. I lie still in the bed in a state of unnerving shock and dismay. Looking through the darkness of the room, I was too afraid to move. Rage pummeled my insides. A white-hot fury burned in my veins. I immediately ran to the shower in tears. I must have stayed in the shower for an hour that night trying to wash the smell of him from my skin. Mostly though, I was scared, confused, angry, and disoriented. I wasn't sure if I should to go tell someone what had happened immediately. Even if I did want to do that, who would I tell at that time of the night? Who should I go to? Was he serious that if I told someone about what had happened, he would kill me?

After finishing my shower, I laid back in my bunk, going over in my head, thinking about what had just happened. I felt traumatized; was the Soldier who'd raped me going to return? I felt his presence in the shadows, lurking. Even if he wasn't there, his silhouette was in my mind. I lay stiff and still in the darkness, soaking in my own tears of shame, guilt and denial, wondering why this happened to me. My roommates returned that night and saw me in tears on my bunk. They keep asking me what was wrong. Was there a family emergency back home? I didn't tell any of them what had happened. I didn't tell anyone for quite some time.

CHAPTER 10

The Courage To Come Forward

In the days and weeks that followed, I wrestled with what had occurred that night. I had fallen into a deep state of depression. I spent a lot of time at the gym working out. I worked out every day, trying to purge myself of what had happened as if the experience of Sexual Assault Trauma would pour out of me through my sweat and tears.

I also grappled with two conflicting feelings. I wanted to talk to someone about the assault. I was grappling with a deep feeling of guilt and shame. I wanted to purge those memories of that night from my mind. I felt dirty from the inside out. My self-esteem was shaken. I didn't know what I'd done to deserve something like this. Over and over in my head, I found myself wondering why that Soldier had picked me to assault. Why me? Were there other Soldiers in the unit he had done this to who were also afraid to come forward?

After the assault, I discovered the Soldier worked in the Military Personnel & Pay Records Section in the unit. This was one of the reasons why I didn't come forward. I worried that he would sabotage my personnel, pay records and not process the paperwork for my next promotion to Private First Class. And so, I kept it all inside.

Instead, I isolated myself on weekdays and weekends staying in the barracks. I grew increasingly distant from the other Soldiers. Newly promoted PFC Jackson and Talarczyk showed concern. They asked me what was wrong. They made jokes about how quiet I'd become. Other Soldiers pulled me aside to ask me if I was okay. I didn't tell them. I couldn't.

Before the Soldier transferred back to the states, I avoided him when I saw him coming, walking in the opposite direction. I avoided walking past the building he worked in. After I found out the Soldier had transferred back to the states, I finally gained the confidence to tell someone. I decided to request a meeting with the Company First Sergeant the next morning. Maybe, if I told the first Sergeant what had happened, I'd feel a little better. Maybe I could start to feel like myself again and break out of this state of depression and guilt.

I requested a meeting with the First Sergeant and carefully planned what I would say.

The First Sergeant agreed to have the meeting with me. I knocked on his door, and he replied: "enter." I walked in and stood at the first sergeant's desk. I bravely stood at the position of parade rest as the First Sergeant gave me the order to stand at ease and to have a seat in the chair in his office. I held my hands together in my lap, and with fear twisting in my belly, I poured out my story. I told the first sergeant what had happened that night, while I was alone in my room in the barracks. I didn't go into a lot of detail. I only told him the basics. I relayed the events of that night, telling the first sergeant about how the Soldier had held a knife and threatened me, how he'd pushed me down onto the bed and forced himself onto me, why I hadn't told anyone because the Soldier told me if I did he would kill me.

I relayed all of this, all while the first sergeant listened carefully, a frown creasing his features, a hand beneath his chin. I talked, thinking that the first sergeant would take my concerns seriously. I thought he would tell me how to move forward and how I could get help with at least my depression, whatever that might mean. But that wasn't the way the conversation went.

When I'd finished speaking, the first sergeant looked at me with deadly serious eyes, the glow of the afternoon light casting an ambient glow throughout the small office.

"PFC Taylor, why did you tell me that?" he asked.

I gaped at him.

"What do you mean, First Sergeant?"

"Exactly what I said, why did you tell me that?"

His eyes were hard, penetrating mine.

"So...so that you could tell me what I needed to do and get some help," I stammered. "I don't know what I'm supposed to do about this. I don't know how to deal with it."

"This is how you deal with it," he replied in a smooth voice. "You forget it ever happened."

My eyes widened. I stared at him. I hadn't been sure what kind of reaction my confession would bring, but I certainly hadn't expected one like this.

"PFC Taylor, I don't know what I'm supposed to make of a story like that," the first sergeant went on, leaning back in his seat and crossing his arms in front of his chest. "How can I believe a story like that? It's downright crazy. The Soldier you're accusing was respected in the unit and battalion. And that kind of thing doesn't happen in the military. It doesn't happen to *Soldiers*. I think you had a bad dream. That's all. Now, be a good a Soldier that you are, and get over your bad dream. I'm not your momma PFC Taylor! Don't come crying to me about nightmares."

A sense of dismay washed over me in a great wave. I could hardly maintain eye contact with the First Sergeant after those comments. As I jumped to my feet and snapped back to parade rest, eyes focused on the first sergeant's black subdued rank on his right shoulder collar, I hastily apologized for wasting his time and asked if I could be dismissed. Tears were pricking in my eyes as I hurried back to my room. I was upset the first sergeant didn't believe me. Again as I said in my introduction, indeed, you may not remember the dates and exact times that it happened to you, but you will always remember three things, what happened to you, where you were and how you felt during the sexual assault. Back then, I remember thinking that maybe the first sergeant was right. Maybe I *was* in the wrong to talk about it. Was it sexual assault? I will be ok. Did I just need to suppress the memory of what happened that one night to regain stability in my life?

Back in the eighties in the armed forces, there was no support system for military sexual assault victims like there is today. Things are better nowadays. There are more resources available, and it is become more acceptable to come forward. There are, however, countless stories that the world will never hear because victims of sexual assault in the military were silenced. It's trauma that doesn't go away. It lingers, pressing in on ones psyche, reverberating through every facet of a person's life. Despite feeling so helpless, I thought I would never be in control of my life again while the attacker went free.

I'll always remember the isolation I felt when I tried to speak up, only to be told to be quiet about it. The first sergeant's statement that this kind of thing *doesn't* happen in the military is false. I can say that it *shouldn't*. But I can also say that it does. Being assaulted by a fellow service member is a horrifying experience. We are supposed to be a team. When someone on your team turns against you in violence, *sexual violence,* it is a terrible betrayal. Soldiers need to be able to rely on their fellow Soldiers to have their back, lean on each other for support and guidance. Soldiers should protect each other. I know that, for me, after talking to the first sergeant, I felt like I'd been betrayed twice, once by my attacker and once by the first sergeant.

Eventually, I knew I would share my story about the assault. I would one day write about the experience. For many years, I kept the assault to myself. Today, I can no longer be silent. Sexual Assault in the military happens to Soldiers, men, and women in uniform. I had to convince myself that I have no reason to feel shame or being in denial. If I had it to do all over, I would have reported the assault to someone in the chain of command that night. You have every right to tell their story. If anyone tries to silence you, that leader or person in your Chain of Command is in the wrong.

There is a compelling quote I'd like to share; "What gives a man the right to violate another man so shamefully? To take away something that cannot be replaced. To destroy a man's future. To take away his manhood. The act seems so small, so insignificant."

As my time in Germany was coming to an end, I prepared for my Permanent Change of Station(PCS) to my next unit, HSC, 268th Aviation Battalion in Fort Lewis Washington and my next promotion to Specialist Fourth Class, I reflected on the last year and a half in Germany. There were some highs and lows, good and bad times. But, there was a bright side to it all. I saw a different side of the world and made some good friends along the way. Lastly, "Auf Wiedersehen"(Goodbye) Germany.

CHAPTER 11

A Mother's Love And Understanding

I returned home to Fayetteville after my overseas assignment in Germany. I was granted another thirty days of leave. I came back home feeling like a different person and Soldier. During the long flight back to the United States, I made the decision to sit down and tell my mother about the sexual assault. When I got home, I passed out souvenirs to the family I had brought back from Germany. Afterwards, I sat down with my mother and told her about the sexual assault. She could already tell there was a sudden change in my mood since I was home on leave after graduation from AIT. My Mother has contributed the following words to this book.

"*While home on leave and rotation from Germany, my son shared the story of his sexual assault with me. I was upset, hurt, and appalled that I'd agreed to send my son to serve his country, and because of that, he'd experienced such a horrible trauma at such a young age. He is so ashamed of it that he never talks about it around his brothers and sisters. He has had to live with this as an Enlisted/Officer Soldier for over thirty-six years. He tells me that he wishes he would have reported the sexual assault sooner, but he worried that other Soldiers in his unit might find out and think he was gay. I witnessed his depression and the changes in his behavior and mood. That is why I told him he needed to get help because I'd heard of Soldiers suffering from PTSD, and thought he might have some of those symptoms as a result of such a Sexual traumatic experience."*

My mother was a great support system for me during this time. She told me she would always love me, offered me comfort, and encouraged me to get help as soon as I could. She helped me to realize that it hadn't been my fault. It hadn't had anything to do with me. The Soldier who attacked me did it because he was a very sick person, and for no other reason than that. He thought he could get away with it. What happened wasn't a result of anything that I did or didn't do. She encouraged me to find a way in my heart to forgive him because that would be the godly thing to do. She said the first sergeant was wrong and gave me bad advice.

Sexual Assault can occur on or off base, during war or peacetime, while a service member is on or off duty. Perpetrators can be men or women, military personnel or civilians, superiors or subordinates. They may be a stranger or a friend. It is an epidemic. **WE,** as victims, need to encourage one another to speak up, get help, and tell our stories. It is never okay for someone else to harass or assault anyone. If your chain of command doesn't want to listen, go and tell some else. Military Sexual Assault is a reality in the armed services, but it doesn't have to be.

When I set out to write a memoir, I knew I had to address my sexual assault. This period of my life was painful. It was definitely a low point of my military career. But I felt my experience was so relevant to share, to encourage others to come forward if they are going through a similar situation. I just want you to know, you're not alone. Life will go on. You will pick yourself back up, and you will feel like yourself again. But it will take time. You will move forward, trust me.

CHAPTER 12

Acceptance And Forgiveness

After my conversation with my mother while home on leave, I thought it was important to include this chapter in the memoir. After all, she encouraged me to find a way to move on and seek closure in this ordeal. My mom was right. I needed to find a way to forgive the Soldier, who assaulted me. From a military standpoint, I had to move on so I could focus on my military career. As months and years passed, I continue to think about that night of the sexual assault differently. I think about the other Soldier. I often wonder if he does regret what he did to me that night? More than likely not. In my head, I thought about what I should have done differently. Slowly, through prayer, all at once, I gave myself permission to let go of it. I acknowledged acceptance, and I realized I can't go back and change what happen that night.

I was an innocent victim. He'd held a knife to my throat. I did everything that I could that night. The burden of this sin is on him, not me. I can't change the past, but I can influence the future. The simple fact is, when something traumatic happens to us, we must piece our lives back together. Yes! I have forgiven him, If I didn't extend my forgiveness to him, it would be like me living the entire experience repeatedly in my head. And, God would not have forgiven me. Whatever my hurt still is, I need to keep that hurt in perspective, knowing that I will never forget. It was a hard road to get to a place where I am today. I have arrived, and I am rejuvenated. It is like a sky of a dark cloud overhead has dissipated. It feels like the sun shining down on me once again. It is like a new beginning. Wow! The power of forgiveness will surely set you free.

CHAPTER 13

The End Of My Enlistment

When my leave ended, I was back on an airplane headed west for what was more than likely I thought was my last assignment in the military. When I arrived at the company area, I met Specialist Rowden. SPC Rowden and I immediately became friends. We both arrived at the company around the same time. We occupied the same room in the barracks. I can always remember SPC Rowden being late to morning formations and having to perform extra duty in the evenings. Other Soldiers in the company would ask me why I hung around SPC Rowden because he was such a loser. I saw much more in him. He may not have been the best Soldier, but he was a great friend and always had my back. I always had his back to. SPC Rowden was a wild rebel. Yes! I remember your theme song was Billy Idol's "Rebel Yell" and you surely lived up to it. SPC Rowden, I hope you find your way to this memoir so we can reconnect. I will never forget our trips to Canada and our squad going to my first concert ever, Elton John, at the Seattle Kingdome. I miss you, man!

The next year passed in a blur. The company went on many field training exercises at the Yakima Military Training Center in Yakima, Washington. The end of my three-year enlistment was approaching. I again, found myself with a decision to make, whether to re-enlist for three more years or go back home to Fayetteville. I guess my plans of being a career Soldier had changed. I must admit, I was terribly homesick. In the back of my mind was still the weight of the Sexual Assault, which I kept hidden and never discussed with anyone while stationed at Fort Lewis. Even though I thought I had moved on, I would find myself still having flashbacks about the attack.

I kept thinking, was it the right decision to go home, just to hit the reset button, unwind, and think about my next chapter in life.

It wasn't an easy decision, though. A huge part of me wanted to go home, but there was another part of me that wanted to stay in the Army. I was torn at the thought of leaving the military behind, letting go of everything I'd worked so hard for the last three years.

I tried to motivate myself to re-enlist in the Army for another three years. If I stayed, it would mean more than likely another assignment in either Germany or Korea. I even auditioned for the Army Band to play drums. I thought getting a new MOS skill would get me excited to re-enlist. I could play drums by ear. I could keep a steady beat. I'd say I sounded pretty good. There was one catch though; I couldn't read sheet music, and the Army Band Sergeant noticed that right away.

He probably noticed it when I didn't look down at the sheet music in front of me during the audition. He gave me a strange look, before asking, "Can you read music?"

I shook my head.

"No, I'm afraid I can't, Sergeant."

There comes a time in life when you must tell the truth and be honest with yourself. The truth was that I was ready for the next phase of my life to begin. I wasn't disappointed when I didn't earn a place in the Army band. One night while in the barracks, I made my decision not to re-enlist. I received my honorable discharge orders from active duty military service and returned home to Fayetteville.

Looking back, I may not have thought my decision through before leaving the army. I had no idea what my next step would be. I considered attending school since I had earned the benefits to go and obtain an associate or bachelor's degree at any college or university I chose. While home, I spent a few weeks getting settled back into the swing of civilian life, enjoying time with my family, helping around the farm. It was no lie I started to missed the army.

It was good to be back home on the farm, to gather my thoughts and reflect on what I had accomplished in the Army for those short three years. The thought did cross my mind that if I re-enlisted, what other opportunities would I have been provided.

I didn't linger in my thoughts for too long. I missed the regimented schedule, strict rules, and military disciplines of the army, I couldn't remain directionless or with no purpose in life for long. I wanted the best of both worlds, to continue to be a part-time citizen Soldier and civilian. So, I re-enlisted in the Tennessee Army National Guard and was later promoted to Sergeant(E5). Enlisting in the National Guard seemed like a good fit for me if I was planning to attend college. The National Guard performs a minimum of one-weekend drill per month and two weeks per year of active duty for training which is also commonly referred to as summer camp. This was a decision I never will regret which lead me to three deployments and a thirty-plus year stint in the full-time Army National Guard.

CHAPTER 14

You Need To Sweep That Floor, Sergeant!

My first drill weekend was with the 1/115th Field Artillery Battery in Shelbyville, Tennessee. The Soldiers in the unit were very welcoming. A couple years later, I was transferred to the Joint Forces Headquarters Command in Nashville, Tennessee. I was assigned as the unit supply specialist. It was not long before I get the opportunity to attend Officer Candidate School in Smyrna, Tennessee, to become a Commissioned Officer. My decision to become an officer was kind of predetermined by one of my mentors. I planned to retire in the Army National Guard as a Command Sergeant Major(CSM).

I would like to share with you how I got the opportunity to go to Officer Candidate School. It was the end of drill weekend at Joint Forces Headquarters. For some reason, the Company Commander and First sergeant were not in a good mood that day and needed someone to sweep the hallway floors. So, they grabbed me to do the honors. I was sweeping the floor when out of nowhere came the Joint Forces Headquarters, Chief of Staff, Colonel "Cooley" B. Wynns, who stopped by and started a conversation with me.

"Why are you sweeping the floor by yourself, Sergeant Taylor," asked the colonel.

I responded with, "Sir, I am just following orders, the company commander and first sergeant told me to do it."

"They can't find a couple of privates to do this, sergeant?" said the colonel.

"Sir, I guess not," I replied.

Shortly, there was a voice that came from the company commander's office.

"Sergeant, who told you to stop sweeping the floor shouted the Commander, you don't have time to talk!"

In a loud and commanding voice, the Colonel said,

"I told Sergeant Taylor to stop sweeping the floor and commander, and if you got a problem with it, then you need to come and finishing sweeping the floor yourself!"

"I tell you what Commander, you come and finish sweeping the floor, Sergeant Taylor, you come with me", said the colonel.

Moments later, I am sitting in the colonel's office.

The colonel asked me,

" Thomas, how would you like to become an Officer?"

"It would mean no more sweeping floors the colonel said with a jokingly smile."

I explained to the colonel that I aspired to move up through the enlisted ranks and retire as a Command Sergeant Major. But Colonel Wynns had already made the decision for me. After a brief conversation over the telephone by Colonel Wynns with the OCS commandant, I was on my way to becoming an officer. I guess Colonel Wynns saw something in me that day I did not see. He knew I could make a more significant impact as an Officer in the Army National Guard and use my previous active-duty enlisted military experience to become a good leader of Soldiers.

I graduated from Officer Candidate School and earned the rank of Second Lieutenant. Shortly After graduation, I attended the Officer Advanced Course at Fort Lee Virginia. Graduating from both schools is one of the highest points of my military career. OCS and OAC involved mental and physical toughness on a somewhat different level.

I received the Most Spirited and Leadership award while attending the Officer Advance Course. At that moment, standing on stage and receiving those awards, I attributed my success to Colonel Wynns. If It weren't for him, I would not have been standing on the stage that day receiving those awards. I am grateful to Colonel "Cooley" Wynns,(Ret.). You forever changed my life that day I was sitting in your office. It just took me a while to recognize it. I still could be sweeping floors in Joint Forces headquarters if it weren't for you. You truly are one of my mentors, at the beginning of my young army officer career.

CHAPTER 15

The First Deployment (Saudi Arabia)

My first assignment as a Second Lieutenant was in the Detachment 1,1175th Quartermaster Company in Lafayette, Tennessee, as a platoon leader. I started out in the detachment with two strikes against me; being black and a brand-new army officer fresh out of school. I struggled to find a way to earn the trust of the Soldiers in the platoon. I wanted to convince them I could be a good leader.

There is normally a platoon sergeant assigned along with squad leaders in the platoon. The platoon sergeant is the subject matter expert and runs the day to day operation of the platoon. As a brand-new Second Lieutenant, you are branded with the nickname (A-DALT) which translates to "A Dumb Ass Lieutenant." This really means you are newly promoted in the officer ranks, and you know absolutely nothing about leading or telling Soldiers what to do. The platoon sergeant was Sergeant First Class (SFC) Carmen B, Hammock. One drill weekend he said to me,

"A-DALT while you in this platoon, this is how it is going to work, I am going to run this platoon."

"All you have to do is stay out of my way, sign documents when I ask you to sign them, and we will get along just fine."

And that is what exactly I did! We made a great team. Thank you for your mentorship and for keeping me out of trouble SFC Hammock,(Ret.).

About ninety days after arriving at the detachment, we received orders to deploy to Saudi Arabia in support of Desert Shield/ Desert Storm. The company's deployment bases were Saudi Arabia and King Khalid Military City (KKMC). I had no idea what to expect, nor did the entire company. Most of the Soldiers in the company had never been out of the United States. I still get emotional today thinking about when we received deployment orders. The Soldiers in the platoon embraced me and accepted me as their platoon leader. I remember them saying to me;

"Sir, we are going to war! It's time to put our war faces on. War sees no color of Soldiers skin. We are now a platoon that is part of a company. We have a mission to do! All of us need to leave home as a team and make it back home as a team. You are our leader now, sir. Let's go, "getter" done!"

Before the company left for the Mobilization Station, the city of Lafayette gave a big send-off. It was a ceremony that I will never forget. The residents lined the streets, bridges, and overpasses, dressed in their red white and blue outfits, proudly waving their American flags as the company military convoy slowly rolled by in serials en-route to the mobilization station.

The company conducted the majority of the deployment training at Fort Campbell, Kentucky. Once again, I packed up my stuff in my two duffel bags, said goodbye to my family, and set out for another big army adventure. The training days leading up to deployment were long and rigorous at times. We were briefed on the country's cultures, language, and expectations, as well as some of the company's responsibilities while in the middle east. There is a lot to preparation in getting a company ready for deployment. Each day was filled with military classes, another stint in the Gas Chamber, weapon, grenade ranges, and equipment training conducted rain or shine.

All Soldier's in the Company underwent physical examinations. To deploy to the middle east, we received anthrax, smallpox shots, and were tested for Tuberculosis (TB). The shots were given early in the morning. They were unlike any shots I'd ever had been given before. While most shots are just a sharp prick and maybe some residual dull soreness afterward, these shots made your arm feel like it was on fire. That's the best way I have of describing it; it was like a liquid fire had been sent flooding through my veins. My arm seared with a white-hot heat, burning from the inside out. Lastly, each Soldier received their ever so popular Desert Pattern Six Colored Combat Deployment Uniforms.

There were loads of equipment that had to prepped, loaded on the rail for transport to the port and be loaded on cargo ships destined to Saudi Arabia. Finally, the day came for the company to depart. I can remember the Fort Campbell Post Commander giving us departure ceremony before we left for Atlanta to depart to Saudi Arabia.

My chest tightened as a team of Soldiers loaded all the duffel bags under the belly of the airplane. The huge jet plane lifted into the clouds. Back over the ocean, I would go this time for another long flight. I was not a complete newbie to overseas travel, as I'd been when I'd first left for Germany. But I was still very nervous. None of us had been to this part of the world. I'd been briefed, but still wondered if I knew enough, if I'd be prepared enough, if the Soldiers in the unit were ready to take on this important mission.

Life in Saudi Arabia was a huge culture shock for all us. I quickly realized Germany was much more like American culture. I'd taken those similarities for granted while living in Germany. But they were obvious to me now that I was deployed to the Middle East. While at Fort Campbell, those debriefing meetings had dragged on for hours, but I was appreciative for them now. I was glad to have been given any information about the middle east which would be home for the 1175th Quartermaster Company for nine months. Back during the Gulf War deployments, deployed forward companies had no clue when they would come home. All that we knew was, we would be deployed until the job was done.

During the first months of deployment, there wasn't a lot of logistical infrastructure in place for units. We lived out of our rucksacks for months or sometimes even longer. Many Soldiers didn't have a hot meal and survived on Meal Ready to Eats(MRE) for thirty days or longer.

But in the end, the Company did accomplish its mission, and all Soldiers made it back home safely. The cities of Carthage and Lafayette, Tennessee threw a massive homecoming celebration for us. As I finish this chapter now, I am in tears. Third Platoon, Det 1, 1175th Quartermaster Company, you guys were the best **DAM** Soldiers I have ever served and deployed with in the desert. Thank you so much for accepting me in your family circle and allowing me to serve as your leader. I will be grateful forever, "Petroleum fuel handler dawgs."

CHAPTER 16

Two More Deployments

Deployment turned out to be the norm for Army National Guard units back then. I learned something different from each deployment. With each mission, I grew as a professional leader and Officer. We are truly blessed in the United States with our freedom and our rights.

My next two deployments were in Support of Operation Iraqi Freedom (2004-2005) with the 230th Area Support Group located in Dyersburg, Tennessee and in (2011-2012) In Support of Operation New Dawn with the 230th Sustainment Brigade, in Millington, Tennessee. Deploying meant more deployment training this go around to different mobilization stations, which included Camp Shelby Mississippi, Fort Bragg, North Carolina and Fort Hood, Texas. With each deployment, the unit had to go through the infamous gas chamber training. I remember mentally bracing myself for the unpleasant ordeal one more time. I could still recall the burning sensation in my lungs and the putrid smell of the CS gas, from my first time in the gas chamber during basic training.

Gas chamber training was slightly different than in boot camp. For one thing, we had to cover ourselves with baby powder so that the sulfur wouldn't burn our skin. The baby powder didn't do much, though. Fortunately, we only had to stay in the chamber for only a few minutes, but it felt much longer. I can recall my friend Major Beard had a worse time of it than any Soldier in the unit because he couldn't get his protective mask to seal properly. While in the gas chamber, he sucked in some major CS gas. When he left the chamber, his face was bright red, and he couldn't stop coughing. I thought he was going to pass out. But all Soldiers made it through the gas chamber in the end.

Most days spent at Fort Bragg were rainy. One day when the weather got so bad, the Post Commander postponed land navigation training. This is very rare for the army to cancel training due to weather. The army doesn't cancel anything due to weather. If it hadn't been for all of the flooding and hurricane warnings, the unit would have been out there training under the torrents of rain, getting soaked down to our bones. As one of the drill sergeants used to say in basic training,

"It never rains *in* the army; it just rains *on* the army."

Most of the deployment training took place under hot and muggy conditions. After a long soaking rain, there was a lot of time spent sloshing through squelching mud. One of the funniest stories during the land navigation course was when, Major Beard was not watching where he was going, lost his footing, slipped and fell right down into a mud hole. His feet flew out from under him, and his rear end hit the mud with a splat. The look of utter shock on his face was something that I will never forget. The rest of the squad cracked up with laughter. Major Beard fumed, looking around at all of us laughing and did not find his mishap as amusing as we did. Even the quietest officer in the unit who never laughed a lot, Lieutenant Colonel Jones, burst into laughter. Major Bead spent the rest of that day pretty irritated, but now it's something that we laugh about today. It is still one of my favorite funny war stories I like teasing the now Colonel Beard,(Ret.), with when we talk over the telephone.

A story Colonel Beard,(Ret.) teases me about is when I purchased a hand-held Global Positioning System (GPS) from the Post Exchange (PX). On one of the unit's days off from training, I got this bright idea to practice land navigation training on my own with my new GPS on the land navigation courses on Fort Bragg. The course was in the woods on the other side of the post. I thought it would be a snap, with my new fancy piece of technology in hand. How could I ever get lost?

Well, it didn't exactly go that way. I started out strong, finding a couple of points on the course with ease, making my way effortless through the deep vegetation on the course. But somehow, I ended up making a wrong turn on the course and got lost. I wandered around in the woods, trying to get back on the right points. I must have walked and walked for hours, panicking as I drifted further in the woods from the base. Later, I found myself at the edge of the forest on the other side of the post, cars passing through the breaks in the trees up ahead. I finally convinced another Soldier to give me a ride back to the unit area. I'd been walking for so long, and I was tired, sweaty, dirty, and exhausted. The Commander and of course my good friend Major Beard had a great big laugh. The Commander gave me the nickname "The Lost GI" during the rest of the deployment.

There were a lot of factors which make any deployment incredibly stressful. You are away from your families for months sometimes up to almost a year. The mission requires you to work seven days a week with very little time off and different work shift hours. We were not allowed to leave the forward deployment bases without our assigned weapon and had to be accompanied by another Soldier. There is not a lot of downtime to unwind from all the stress of the workday. The weather was a battle all on its own. The days were long and hot, with constant sandstorms which came out from nowhere. The convoys into Iraq were very long and dangerous. A security detail traveled with each convoy, searching for and sometimes disarming improvised explosive devices (IEDs) along the route.

During my three deployments to South West Asia, I did learn that not everyone has the same values as America. Countries outside of the Western world have a long history of culture and ethics that aren't built on the tenets of democracy. They don't draw on the foundations as the western world does. They prioritize different things. This isn't a judgment; it's simply a fact.

Many of the civilians that I got to know were afraid to see the military leave. They knew that we were their allies. This, for me, validates the fact we did help those people, giving those citizens some comfort, reassurance, and support meant so much to me personally. This is one of the good things about serving in the military. It's about service, not only to serve one's country, but all the people that we interact with during the mission. I hope that during support of these operations deployments, the military won the hearts and minds of people in South West Asia. The media, however, can sometimes focus so much on the violence and oppression of the war environment instead of the humanitarian efforts provided by the military. Human beings are resilient and hopeful creatures, and even in the darkest of situations, there is light. I am living proof. The light of humanity shines bright, even from the most shadowed and shattered corners of the globe.

Most importantly, when Soldiers deploy, camaraderie is the most essential thing for mission accomplishment. You need to have a bond with your fellow Soldiers and the unit. This is

the cornerstone of the military. It's where the military derives its strength from. You've got to be able to lean on each other. During deployment, You need your fellow Soldiers, and they need you.
   `

CHAPTER 17

The Reality Of War

I would have not made it through three deployments without the letters, phone calls, care packages, and support from back home.

You make a lot of friends during deployment, Sadly, after the units return home from deployment, friendships end due to Soldiers leaving or retiring from the military to spend time with their families.

But nothing is more painful than the death of a fellow Soldier, friend during combat operations. The reality is this happens during war. I remember serving as a Causality Assistance Officer(CAO) for a Soldier. A Casualty Assistance Officer's function is to notify the survivor when a service member has died. Being a CAO was one of the toughest assignments of my military career, but also, at the same time a tremendous honor. You are there twenty-four-seven to ensure the survivor's immediate needs are met during this difficult time. There are no easy words to say to the survivors to comfort them. You must be there for them until the survivors feel that your assistance is no longer needed or desired. To all the Fallen Soldiers, Sailor's, Marines, Coast Guard, Airmen, and civilians, who paid the ultimate sacrifice for our freedom,to those honorable Soldiers and their families, I thank you each day. I would like to end this chapter with a quote from Winston Churchill,

"We sleep soundly in our beds because rough men stand ready in the night to visit violence on those who would do us harm." We will never forget!

CHAPTER 18

Transition Back To Civilian Life

It is often said that everything in life has a beginning, middle, and ending. The Army is not any different. After years of serving my country, many military assignments, making close friends, traveling the world, and deploying to various countries around the globe, it was finally time for me to hang up the uniform. It was time to close this chapter in my army life and start a new chapter, transitioning back to civilian life.

I've heard many a service member says it; 'The Army doesn't retire, you do!' Transitioning back to civilian life from the military comes with a lot of unique challenges. For everyone who is continuing to serve, this is by far one of the most important transition you will ever make.

Reverend T.D. Jakes says, "Throughout your life, you have to experience it, enjoy it, survive it, endure it, handle it, and go through it." These words ring true in all situations, but I find they're especially applicable to those preparing for any phase of life.

As you move into military retirement, it's important to have a written plan. Be prepared to rewrite that plan as required and be flexible. Organization is the key to a smooth re-entry to civilian life. A written plan gives you a sense of structure as you leave the military life behind. No matter how precise and exacting a plan is, murphy's law has a way of setting in at the most inconvenient moments.

For me, I found this out the hard way three weeks into my transition. I had flown back to Nashville, Tennessee when my family was hit with a crisis. My sister became very ill. She was diagnosed with Necrotizing Fasciitis. This is a rare and severe flesh-eating bacteria. Her symptoms were severe, and she nearly died. This was a tough time for my family. The family banded together to support my sister in her sickness and prayed for her swift recovery. Thankfully, she pulled through. We were immensely grateful to see her regain her strength. God is an amazing God!

This is what I meant by being flexible. It is always important to remember when life happens, the family is always the most important before anything. My mother would always say to us; "put God and family first, everything else will fall into place and it always does.

Finding a job post-military can be hard. Military Occupational Skills (MOS) skills and invaluable core values learned from the military such as Loyalty, Duty, Respect, Selfless Service, Honor, Integrity, and personal courage don't always translate easily into the civilian sector.

Communicating your MOS skills to a prospective employer without the use of military jargon was difficult for me. You must present your military skills sets to an employer in a way that makes sense for them to understand. Applying for jobs requires writing resumes, cover letters, networking, lots of research on job sites on the internet and interviewing.

The other big shock that comes with retiring is the cost of living. Retirement turned out to be a lot more expensive than I'd ever thought it would be. During my time in the army, Uncle Sam paid for three square meals a day, put a roof over my head, and uniforms.

Going back to a life of bills and expenses can be jarring. My advice is to take charge of your finances early and invest in yourself while you are young. Let your money work for you. When you get paid, pay yourself first and start investing early. Delay instant gratification in your earlier years. Trust me, the when you want it; and I want it now mentality is not the way to go throughout your military career. Attend financial management classes on post if offered, so you can educate yourself about the rules of money, how money works and do not take on any new debt. It is a good idea to be debt-free when you retire from the military. .

Then there's the challenge of trying to figure what you really want to do after retiring from the military. In the military, your career is pretty much laid out. You move up the ranks going from enlisted ranks of Private to Command Sergeant Major, or from the officer ranks Second Lieutenant to General. Another avenue you can explore when leaving the military is starting your own business. That is the path that I took. Even after retirement, the army provided me the opportunity to obtain the education needed to start my business. Thanks to the military, I was allowed to attend Audio Engineering, Music Business, and The Academy of Radio &TV Broadcasting classes. With the education I gained from these classes, I launched my own Production and Indie Record Company, "Igotyoursixx Productions and Dance Therapee Records." I also launched my own Internet Radio Station, "Dance Therapee Radio." I host a weekly podcast entitled "The Music Nation Podcast." I started a foundation called "Keeping Our Veterans Off the Street" and will soon launch my own YouTube Channel. I love supporting good causes by riding in charitable bicycle rides. My goal is to pick up a side hustle to generate more income to support, advertise, and promote my business instead of taking out small business loans and incurring more debt.

What I am finding out in the civilian workforce, there is a different mindset than in the military. The civilian workplace is much more individualistic and competitive. People are still expected to work together, but the level of teamwork isn't the same. You don't worry about the *esprit de corps* of the team as much as you worry about the good of your own career, inflated bonuses, and your personal advancement through the company.

When you retire, the lack of structure can be challenging to get used to. I was used to wearing a uniform and combat boots for the past Thirty-six years. I don't have set meal times. I can eat whenever I want. I don't have strict schedules or someone telling me exactly where I needed to be, each hour of the day. As silly as it might sound to those who haven't been in the army, that lack of structure is sometimes needed trust me to keep your sanity. I had to get back to picking out a different shirt every day, deciding when to have lunch, and doing everything from making small daily decisions to imagining what the rest of my life would be like. I advise anyone making this transition, to make a point of creating your own structure. Decide what your schedule will look like. You can't go from all structure to no structure in a snap. Like everything, it takes time. It really is the little things that go such a long way and keep you going every day after the Army.

I was very fortunate, When I retired from the military, I was blessed to have the opportunity to go back to school.

I will always be grateful for what the military provided my family and me. The military taught me that you can be anything and do anything you want. It does not matter about your age, religion, skin color, or ethnic background. All it takes is hard work and determination. Working hard will always serve you well. I know I did the right thing by serving. The life of a Soldier is a life worth living, and I'm proud to have lived mine. As I look back on my military career, I have no regrets, I happened to think a Job well-done Soldier!

Conclusion

Thank you, from the bottom of my heart, for taking the time to read my story. I've gained immeasurable insights and valuable skills from my time as a Soldier in the army. For those who are thinking about enlisting, I encourage you to go for it "be all you can be" Army Strong! There is so much to be gained and so much to be given. Military service allows you to give back to others in a significant way, not just monetarily. The United States Military helps people around the world. As a member of any one of the service branches, you are the first humanitarian lifeline, providing support and resources to people who need them most. You represent your country, and that is a great honor.

I served my country for thirty-six years. I wouldn't change that for anything. I have no regrets, but fond memories, sad and funny war stories to tell for the rest of my life. When I first saw that Airforce recruiting commercial, I thanked God for opening that door for me. And, I also thanked God for closing that door for when I did not score high enough on the ASVAB to enlist in the air force and then opening another door for me to enlist in the army.

Before my father passed away with a diagnosis from leukemia cancer in 1996, he told me how much he was proud of me. That meant the world to me. I do admit, it took time for him to come to terms with me enlisting in the military. Having my families support behind me, gave me the foundation that

I needed to keep going in the toughest moments and to even write this memoir.

I can't forget to mention one special friend who has been there and supported me through all my army career, Kevin Sollinger. You have been like a brother to me and will always be a special part of my family. Thanks for taking care of the home front while I was deployed and away for extended military missions. You are indeed a godsend. I have always admired your thankless service as a nurse, taking care of the elderly, our aging, and disabled veterans. Thank you!

To all the service members, I met in the other branches of the armed forces and coalition forces, I want to say a special thanks to you and your friendship. In the military, everybody needs a sponsor or a Mentor. My mentors who have since retired were, General Colin Powell, (Ret.), Colonel "Cooley" B. Wynns,(Ret.), Colonel David R. Bates,(Ret.), Colonel Helen Rogers,(Ret.) and SFC Carmon B. Hammock,(Ret.) you all impacted my army career in a significant way.

For all the friendships I have made in the army, there are so many to mention. I'm thankful and will never forget you. The military is like a family; Once a Soldier, Always a Soldier!

If you are thinking about enlisting in the Army or any branch of the Armed Forces, I urge you to pursue it. Both the Airforce and Army recruiters were right. You will get to see the world. You will learn about your strengths, weakness, and what you are really made of. If a shy and introverted boy from Fayetteville, Tennessee, can do it, so can you.

Becoming a Soldier is not easy! Not everyone has what it takes. Becoming a Soldier takes sacrifice, dedication, determination. And, now that my army career has come to an end, I enter my next chapter in life, I have a new mission to conquer on my own terms and to seize every opportunity that is afforded to me. Opportunities are seldom and most often do not knock at your door twice regardless of whatever career path you pursue . I'll always be proud of what I accomplished during my time in the army. I have been fortunate to have many "aha moments" during my army career. And, now I want to have more "aha" moments in my next journey. This is my story, about Life, Resilience, and Success while serving as a Soldier in the Army. It can be your story too. Call a recruiter today. Do some research and begin *your* Soldier's story. If you're like me decades from now, you might just find yourself looking back over a career that gives you incredible pride that you wore the U.S. Army Uniform. My mission is complete. About Face! *HooAh*! Lieutenant Colonel Thomas E. Taylor,(Ret.).

THE END

Printed in Dunstable, United Kingdom